LUFTWAFFE AT WAR

Messerschmitt Bf 109 in the West, 1937–1940

Franz Jaenisch, a young pilot in 3./JG 2 Richthofen is greeted by his comrades at the end of his hundredth war flight. His aircraft, yellow 8, carried his personal emblem, an adaptation of the popular Mickey Mouse with boxing gloves. On 15 October 1940, another pilot, *Feldwebel* Horst Hellriegel, had to force-land this machine (W.Nr 1588) on the Isle of Wight at Bowcombe Down. (*Franz Jaenisch*)

Messerschmitt Bf 109 in the West, 1937–1940

From the Spanish Civil War to the Battle of Britain

Michael Payne

Greenhill Books
LONDON

Stackpole Books
PENNSYLVANIA

Greenhill Books

Messerschmitt Bf 109 in the West, 1937–1940
first published 1998
by Greenhill Books, Lionel Leventhal Limited,
Park House, 1 Russell Gardens,
London NW11 9NN
and
Stackpole Books, 5067 Ritter Road, Mechanicsburg,
PA 17055, USA

British Library Cataloguing in Publication Data

Payne, Michael
Messerschmitt Bf 109 in the West, 1937–1940. –
(Luftwaffe at war; v. 5)
1. Messerschmitt 109 (Fighter planes) – History
2. World War, 1939–1945 – Aerial operations, German
I. Title
940.5'44'943
ISBN 1-85367-305-6

Library of Congress Cataloging-in-Publication Data

Payne, Michael
Messerschmitt Bf 109 in the West, 1937–1940/ by
Michael Payne.
    p.   cm. – (Luftwaffe at war; v. 5)
ISBN 1-85367-305-6
1. World War, 1939–1945 – Aerial operations,
German.
2. Messerschmitt 109 (Fighter planes). I. Title.
II. Series: Luftwaffe at War; v.5.
D787.P32 1998   97-38291
940.54'4943 – DC21   CIP

Designed by DAG Publications Ltd
Designed by David Gibbons
Layout by Anthony A. Evans
Printed in Singapore

MESSERSCHMITT BF 109 IN THE WEST, 1937–1940

Since it was ultimately at the hands of the Royal Air Force that the Messerschmitt Bf 109 met its match over south-eastern England in the autumn of 1940, a suitable starting point for this narrative is 4 May 1940 when Flight Lieutenant Hilly-Brown of No. 1 Sqn flew the Emil W.Nr 1304 across from France for performance trials at A&AEE Boscombe Down to be compared with a Spitfire, a Hurricane, a Curtiss Hawk 75A and a Gloster F5/34. Until the written report by Morien Morgan and Morris emerged in September, the Air Ministry and, more importantly, the pilots of Fighter Command really knew very little about the technical details of the *Luftwaffe*'s front-line fighter.

In March 1936 when the prototype Spitfire first flew, the second example of the Bf 109 (D+IUDE) was already on test, and a series of *Versuch* models followed quickly into the test programme with Jumo 210 motors, and then in 1937 with Daimler-Benz DB 600 and 601 engines. German propaganda always implied that large numbers of Bf 109s were in *Luftwaffe* service. Two machines in service camouflage performed at Zurich-Dübendorf in July 1937 and a sole example had flown over the German Olympics in 1936. The fact remains that no one in London really knew what was happening in Germany.

In fact, the airframes for the early production versions (B, C and D) were subcontracted to Fieseler at Kassel, Erla at Leipzig and Focke-Wulf at Bremen, while a factory and airfield were built at Regensburg to mass-produce the type by the Messerschmitt company.

In July 1936, civil war erupted in Spain. Since the USSR sent war material to support the Republican faction, Hitler and Mussolini sent material and men to help General Franco's Nationalists. For the infant *Luftwaffe*, Spain became a most instructive area where carpet bombing, ground-attack and fighter combat techniques could be developed. *Luftwaffe* personnel were shipped to Spain as civilians in considerable numbers. A significant force of aircraft was dispatched, some flying via Italy and others going by sea to Vigo and Seville. There were He 111s, Do 17s, Ju 52s, Henschel Hs 123s, Me 108s and a number of He 51C biplane fighters drawn from *Luftwaffe* reserves in Germany. These latter were formed into the *Staffeln* of J 88, where they were eventually to be replaced by Bf 109s.

The next important date for the Bf 109 was December 1936 when three of the V models were sent to Spain for evaluation 'in the field'. Among the experienced pilots detailed to fly them operationally was *Oberleutnant* Hannes Trautloft who painted his green heart emblem below the cockpit. Gradually, more Bf 109s reached J 88, at first the Jumo-powered Bs, Cs and Ds. It was not until December 1938 that the Emils began to arrive.

In December 1937, *Feldwebel* Polenz's Bf 109B (coded 6-15) fell into Republican hands. The French were invited to examine it but the report submitted by the test pilot was never shared with London. So while Werner Mölders and his comrades developed skills and tactics in combat over Spain, Whitehall continued to ignore the warnings about German rearmament while Hurricanes and Spitfires trickled out of British factories as though there had never been a Munich Crisis. In September 1939, Gladiator biplanes were sent to France as a part of the British forces.

Meanwhile in Germany, the obsolete biplane fighters were being replaced in the *Gruppen* by Bf 109s. Early subtypes served to introduce the pilots to closed cockpits, flaps, retractable undercarriages and higher wing loadings. Inevitably, there were many accidents. A few of the first Bf 109s to reach Spain had been drawn from existing *Gruppen*. Gradually, later subtypes came into service as the *Luftwaffe* expanded. Units were renumbered in a most confusing manner — far too complicated to describe here — and eventually the production of Daimler-Benz DB 601 motors gained momentum so that the units received the first of the Emils. They began to form an Order of Battle with the designations that came to be familiar during the war — JG 2, JG 3, JG 26. Some units remained as single autonomous *Gruppen* but in the course of time these units joined up with others in order that most *Geschwader* should have a *Stab* and three *Gruppen*.

As an example of this process I./JG 1, which had been formed at Jesau in East Prussia, became associated with the two *Gruppen* of JG 27 until during July 1940 it was redesignated III./JG 27. Historians will realise that this accounts for the aircraft of the third *Gruppe* carrying their numerals on their engine cowlings as had been the custom of JG 1. Another anomaly in the markings system was when I./JG 76 became II./JG 54. The Gruppe carried no bar markings on rear fuselages.

In March 1939, men of the *Legion Condor* came home. Many of the fighter pilots preserved the emblems from J 88 on their aircraft as personal markings. All the Bf 109s that survived in Spain had been given over to the new Spanish Air Force which revised their markings. A number of pilots in 1939–40 painted top hats below their cockpits (Strümpell, Kroeck, Knüppel); others used variations on the Mickey Mouse emblem, such as Jaenisch, Hubertus von Bonin and Adolf Galland.

Werner Mölders, who had gained the highest number of victories among the German pilots, addressed a report to the German Air Ministry (RLM) on the new ideas about fighter tactics that he and his comrades had evolved for the modern types of fighter aircraft. The principle of the two-man *Rotte* and the four-man *Schwarm* had been proved in combat where each pilot in the loose formation was able to cover the others, and all four men flew as a unit. Events in the air happened very quickly; combats might last only seconds and it was Mölders' aggressive doctrine that secured the early successes of the Bf 109.

From the outbreak of war, the real performance of the Bf 109 was unknown by the Allies. After its brief campaign in Poland, the *Luftwaffe* settled down to a policy of equipping every fighter unit with Emils (Bf 109E) while the earlier models were relegated to fighter-pilot training schools (JFS). A fighter force was based in northern Germany to defend Heligoland and the Bight but most of the fighters were deployed behind the Siegfried Line where, during the *Sitzkrieg* (Phoney War), a steady series of skirmishes took place. Reconnaissance aircraft were intercepted regularly by both sides and many were shot down. Several Bf 109s came down in France. In late September, a red 9 of 2./JG 71 came down near Nancy and *Unteroffizier* Georg Pavenzinger was taken prisoner. This Emil crashed while being flown by the French and it was *Feldwebel* Karl Hier's white 1 of 1./JG 76 which survived to be flown to England in May 1940. It had come down on 22 November at Wörth (Bas-Rhin), allegedly in bad visibility.

For the Air Staff of the RAF, December 1939 was a time of decision. When formations of Wellingtons had tried to bomb the German Navy in daylight they had been cut to pieces by the defending fighters. Heavy bombers operated almost entirely at night from 1940. It also came to be realised, though not publicly admitted, that the *Luftwaffe* had a system of radio location (later called radar).

At this period, most of the Emils in service were E-1s which were relatively underarmed with only four 7.9 mm MG 17 machine-guns. A motor cannon had been intended to fire through the hollow propeller shaft but problems had arisen and despite popular belief no operational Emil has ever been found fitted with this cannon. So, compared with the eight-gun Spitfires and Hurricanes the E-1 was inferior in fire-power. However, the E-3 was coming into use with its pair of wing-mounted MG FF 20 mm cannon. With this armament, the

Bf 109E-3 could outrange and outgun the RAF fighters. Cannon fire could devastate the thin-gauge skin and structure of an aircraft.

Other improvements were made, either on production lines or by the units themselves. Furthermore, as airframes went to the Repair Centres some modifications were made which altered the subtype designation; for example, the cannon might be replaced with MG FF M type which fired improved ammunition and in effect turned an E-3 into an E-4. The fitting of the new 'square' hood did not alter the designation. Many Emils were given the later hood which conferred a better view by eliminating the framing at the pilot's eye-level and was more roomy, especially when head armour was added. All Emils were fitted with a two-piece armour bulkhead at frame No. 3 aft of the fuel tank. It was not until well into 1940 that some airframes were given the uprated DB 601N motor. These Bf 109E-4/Ns could be identified by the numeral 100 in the fuel marker; the motor used 100-octane fuel.

On 10 April 1940, German forces moved into Denmark and an airborne and seaborne invasion of Norway was mounted. The Emils of II./JG 77 played a vital part in this operation which the RAF was powerless to prevent owing to the lack of RAF long-range fighters. The Emils picked off the Hudsons, Sunderlands and Blenheims over the sea and the Navy operated only in the far north. The Gladiators of No. 263 Sqn fought valiantly from a frozen lake but without spares and support they were doomed. Hurricanes too were landed (No. 46 Sqn) but the Emils controlled the key areas and the Hurricanes were all lost on the ill-fated HMS *Glorious*.

Meanwhile, an even fiercer conflict was in full flow across northern Europe. On 10 May, German forces attacked in the west. There were two related attacks, both of which were covered by Emils either escorting bombers or on free-chase sorties. First, a strong force moved into the Low Countries as Hitler explained 'in order to protect these neutrals from Allied aggression'. As the BEF and the French moved to meet this threat, an unexpected armoured force crossed the Meuse near Sedan and fanned out across France to strike north-west. German columns reached the Channel coast near the mouth of the Somme, effectively sealing off the BEF which had to be evacuated, mostly across the beaches of Dunkirk. Battles and Blenheims waged a losing struggle to stem the tide but the Emils were everywhere. On 17 May, for example, 1./JG 3 destroyed a complete force of thirteen Blenheims near St Quentin without loss to themselves. Hurricanes claimed successes but in the retreat a huge number of aircraft had to be abandoned.

On 6 June during Operation 'Paula' aimed at installations in the Paris area, Werner Mölders, *Kommandeur* of III./JG 53, was shot down near Chantilly and made prisoner. Following the Armistice at the end of June he and many other prisoners were set free to return to Germany. There ensued an ominous lull in the air. In London, Winston Churchill rallied the nation, the Local Defence Volunteer force was formed and in the first days of July the Battle of Britain began over the Dover Strait.

The Bf 109 units stood down and went on leave for a few days. New pilots joined the old hands. The aircraft were carefully serviced and updated. Elements of JG 51 began to operate from the Pas-de-Calais, while JG 2 provided defence in the west to discourage the RAF from bombing Cherbourg and Brest. When the Stukas began dive-bombing Channel shipping there were always Emils lurking above, waiting to pounce on the RAF fighters.

The limited range of the Emils made it essential to establish airfields near the coast. *Luftflotte* 3 in the west used Maupertus, Dinan, Querqueville and Guernsey, and new strips were made at Crépon, Plumetot and Carquebut. *Luftflotte* 2 established a number of new strips behind Wissant and Cap Griz-Nez, where traces of their occupation can still be found today around Audembert and Marquise. The Channel Tunnel terminal has obliterated the old field at Coquelles and the railway tracks bisect one of JG 54's strips near Guines.

Narratives of the Battle of Britain are quite plentiful but some aspects relative to the Bf 109s merit further comment. First, the camouflage colours. In 1939, the very dark greens (70 and 71) had favoured concealment on the ground, especially among trees. With the prospect of a more mobile campaign in 1940 the greens were altered to green 71 and grey 02 and the fuselage side areas were painted pale blue for sunlight and open countryside. There were exceptions, such as the darker finishes found in JG 53; but in general the Bf 109s began operating across the Channel in pale colours. Soon the bright blue areas acquired a grey-green mottle in various styles for concealment while flying over water. Fighter Command adopted similar colours in 1941 for cross-Channel operations.

Next, the tactics. *Luftwaffe* commanders made a major error in tying the fighters to close escort for bomber formations. The Emil's forte was its free-chase aggression and to deny this to the experienced *Jagdflieger* was not only to misuse the Emil but also to generate frustration and resentment among the pilots. Furthermore, it was a most surprising omission which failed to develop a practical drop tank to extend the Emil's range as soon as it became clear that it would have to operate across the Channel. The Heinkel He 51s had carried them over Spain and the Ju 87s used them in 1940 but the earliest report of an Emil with a tank occurred on 30 November when Wägelein and Schmidt of JG 53 were brought down over Dungeness. The tank was said to leak.

Finally, the bomb-carrying programme. Most unpopular among the pilots, this development decreed that one *Staffel* in each *Gruppe* should train its pilots to operate as fighter-bombers. In the event, most of the pilots got rid of their load as quickly as possible; there was no strategic gain by the *Luftwaffe* whose bomber force, by late October, was already operating mostly after dark. There were two units which had been dedicated to fighter-bomber (*Jabo*) tactics. These were 3/*Erprobungsgruppe* 210 under Otto Hintze and II(*Schlacht*)/LG 2, a *Gruppe* which uniquely marked its Bf 109E-4/Bs with a black triangle behind the cockpit and with letters on the rear fuselage in the standard *Staffel* colours of white, black or yellow. In order that pilots could dive at the correct angle to release the bomb, a thin red line was painted at 45° on the side glazing of the cockpit hood and this could be lined up with the horizon.

As autumn advanced, the landing grounds became waterlogged and the style of the Battle began to change. Prisoners revealed that some units were short of serviceable machines. But *Hauptmann* Hans Asmus has recorded that another change was in the air. On 25 October when he became a prisoner he had been flying in the *Stabskette* of JG 51 with Werner Mölders who had just been provided with a brand new Bf 109F. This was the subtype which would supersede the Emil in most of the *Geschwader* in 1941. Visually, the new Friedrich had a cantilever tailplane, rounded wing-tips and a motor-cannon firing through a large spinner. There were, of course, many other modifications but most importantly it was to prove itself more than a match for the Spitfire until the advent of the Mark V. In its 'clean' form it was considered to be the most pleasant version to fly.

In the course of the Battle of Britain, quite a few Emils had made successful forced landings in southern England. Most of these were photographed and some were put on public display. It was from a study of these machines that historians have been able to learn about the colours, markings, emblems and badges displayed by each unit. No account of the Bf 109 in the first two years of the war can be complete without some pictures taken on the English side of the Channel.

Some *Luftwaffe* camouflage paint colours 1937–40

02 *Grau* A light-grey tone with a green element, towards sage-green.

63 *Grau* A much paler grey, not unlike RAF medium sea grey.

65 *Hellblau* Very pale blue used mainly for undersurfaces.

70 *Schwarzgrün* A very dark green, easily mistaken for black in photographs.

71 *Dunkelgrün* A paler tone of the same 'family' as 70.

74 *Dunkelgrau* Grey used as upper surface camouflage or mottle.

75 *Grau* A lighter tone of grey used with 74.

76 *Weissblau* Pale blue used for under surfaces. Paler than 65 and used with grey tones rather than green.

Below: An aircraft of the *Stab* flight of III./JG 51 during the hot weather of May or June 1940 being refuelled in an uncut field of hay. Note the *Winkel-Kreis* which signifies a Technical Officer. In later months, the *Gruppe* badges (the Axe of Nieder-Rhein) below the cockpits were covered by the mottled camouflage that was sprayed over fuselage sides to make the aircraft less visible on the ground. (*Creek*)

Left: This is an early Bf 109, either a B or a C, with a Jumo engine and a two-bladed propeller. Its camouflage and markings have been updated to a 1940 standard. Many such subtypes found their way into training schools (with yellow tail bands) or were used as hacks for senior officers, like this one. A group of *Hitlerjugend* appear to be enjoying an airfield visit, just as British ATC cadets have done with the RAF.

Below left: As the cross-Channel air activity began to wind down in November 1940, JG 53 bade farewell to von Cramon-Taubadel, as von Maltzahn was promoted to *Geschwader-kommodore*. From 22 November, the unit's *Pik-As* emblem reappeared on the yellow cowlings of their new Bf 109E-7s. Based at Le Touquet and Berck, and equipped to carry drop tanks, most of the new aircraft had capped spinners.

Below: The key to the identity of this Emil lies in the bulge below the fuselage which holds the reconnaissance camera equipment. It is probably an E-5 since it used 87-octane fuel as indicated by the 87 in the triangle. The black numerals have white outlines and the finish is grey 76 rather than the earlier pale blue 65. The machine is probably from 2./AufklGr 13.

Above: Pilots and aircraft of II./JG 54. The white tip on the spinner suggests they are of 4 *Staffel*, of which *Oberleutnant* Hans Philipp (centre) was *Staffelkapitän*. The yellow cowling and rudder, painted with Philipp's victory claims, date the photo as post-August 1940. The style of camouflage is typical of II./JG 54. The *Gruppe* was based a few miles south of Guines.

Opposite page, top: *Oberleutnant* Hermann Seegatz, of JG 5 in Norway, with his black 3. It is an E-7 fitted with a drop tank. The colours in the old photograph have aged badly; the eagle badge below the cockpit was originally red and white. The badge suggests a connection with *Oberleutnant* Pomaska who was shot down and killed over France on 1 June 1940 while leading 6./JG 26. The eagle was his personal emblem.

Right: This photograph was taken at the height of summer when the *Gruppen* of JG 53 were based around the Norman–Breton border — Rennes, Dinan, Cherbourg. Black 3 has a red spinner and a red band round its cowling. *Gefreiter* Heinrich Zag came down near Goudhurst in a 3 of 8. *Staffel* but probably not the same machine as this one. Camouflage and crosses are typical of the third *Gruppe*.

Right: A cold November morning at Le Touquet, or Berck, as 7/JG 53 prepare to take off on a cross-Channel sweep. Note the newly applied *Pik-As* badges, and the custom of painting narrow white corners on III *Gruppe*'s fuselage crosses, making them almost identical to those on the upper wing surfaces. White 2 has no swastika on its fin.

Below: In the centre of this photo is *Major* Werner Mölders, *Kommodore* of JG 51, surrounded by some of his ground crews, and all gathered beside his new aircraft, a Bf 109F-2. Note how the yellow engine cowlings are open, the revised, rounded air intake above the left-hand panel, and the yellow rudder with the rows of victory bars. These did not include his fourteen claims while he was with the *Legion Condor* in Spain. (*C. Goss*)

Opposite page, bottom: As Werner Mölders walks away after the group photo, the yellow rudder of his Friedrich with the sixty-five victory bars is clearly visible. In the background is an older Emil with its yellow cowling and rudder, and with the buzzard badge in its circular patch on the nose. This was the *Geschwader* emblem. (*C. Goss*)

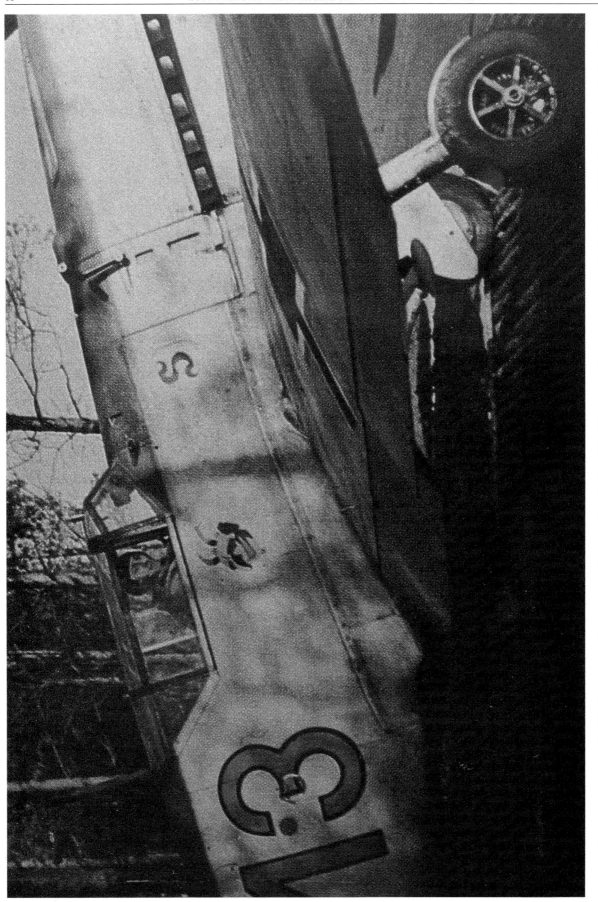

Above: It was the custom of 2./JG 26 to retain the red numerals when all other 'red' *Staffeln* changed their numerals to black. The *Staffel* badge of the devil's head was later moved to the sides of the engine cowling. It was a red 2 of this *Staffel*, flown by *Unteroffizier* Heinz Wolf, that was captured in November 1940 and sent to South Africa where it is now exhibited in the Saxonwold Museum.

Above: The first Bf 109 sent to Spain in December 1936 and flown by Hannes Trautloft. Confusion exists over its identity but it was probably the fourth machine built (V-4). Note the green heart badge below the cockpit. It is coded 6-1 on its pale grey finish. It is uncertain whether it remained in Spain or was shipped back to Germany. (*Arraez Cerda*)

Below: *Hauptmann* Werner Mölders with the Bf 109D that he flew in Spain. He took over the command of 3./J 88 from Adolf Galland in May 1938 and led the *Staffel* until December. Note the Mickey Mouse *Staffel* badge plus the lack of radio mast or aerial on this early Bf 109. The black disc markings on the upper and lower wing surfaces have white diagonal crosses but the fuselage discs were usually plain black unless the pilot marked it with his personal emblem. (*Arraez Cerda*)

Above: During the final months of the Spanish Civil War the first *Staffel*, under Siebelt Reents, introduced this black and white badge — *Der Holzauge*. This Emil, coded 6-89, was flown by *Unteroffizier* Gerhardt Halupczok. He later called himself Herzog and it was with this name that he flew in 2./JG 26 and was taken prisoner on 11 May 1940, the second day of operations over the Low Countries. (*D. Caldwell*)

Below: According to historian Paul Whelan, 6-125 was an E-3, though the bulge below the wing for the 20 mm magazine is not apparent. Upper surfaces are grey 63 with black areas to disguise exhaust fouling. Under surfaces are pale blue 65. The black and white *Holzauge* badge signifies that it is from 1./J 88. Note the wing markings on the photo-machine.

Above: On the left are Bf 109s of *Jagdgruppe* 102; on the far left is *Hauptmann* Hannes Gentzen's machine. Centre right is an elderly Junkers 34 with its wing markings covered with sheets. Beyond is a Ju 87 Stuka and in the distance a Ju 52. The airfield is at Speyer and the date early in 1940. Gentzen was an ace from the Polish campaign and he was to die on 26 May 1940 in a take-off accident. (*J. C. Verrycken*)

Below: Emils of II./JG 26 Schlageter on the edge of a temporary landing ground during *Luftwaffe* war-games prior to the outbreak of war. They are in the very dark greens (70 and 71) of the 1939 camouflage finish and two of the aircraft have their tails marked with white tactical paint. White 1 of 4 *Staffel* in the foreground is probably *Oberleutnant* Ebbighausen's machine. (*J. C. Verrycken*)

Above: Winter 1939 and the colours and markings of the Bf 109s were all being changed. The very dark greens gave way to one dark green (71) and a paler grey-green (02) with the undersides pale blue (65) being drawn up the fuselage sides. Crosses carried wider white edges and gradually swastikas were repainted on the fins. *Stab* markings became a lot more visible.

Opposite page, top: Bf 109E-1, W.Nr 3326, red 9 of 2./JG 71 (later redesignated 2./JG 51) made a good landing in France on 28 September 1939, less than a month after war broke out. *Unteroffizier* Georg Pavenzinger was made prisoner and his aircraft was test-flown by the French until it was destroyed in a mid-air collision. It is possible to see how, in pre-war times, the swastika had been presented on a white disc, set in a broad horizontal red band.

Right: *Oberleutnant* Hans von Hahn's aircraft with its *Adjutant Stabwinkel*, his cockerel emblem on the cowling and the camouflage and markings in the regular style of the pre-war *Luftwaffe*. From this photograph it is easy to understand why most observers at that time believed the German fighters were painted either plain dark green or black. There was, in fact, a two-tone pattern of greens (70 and 71).

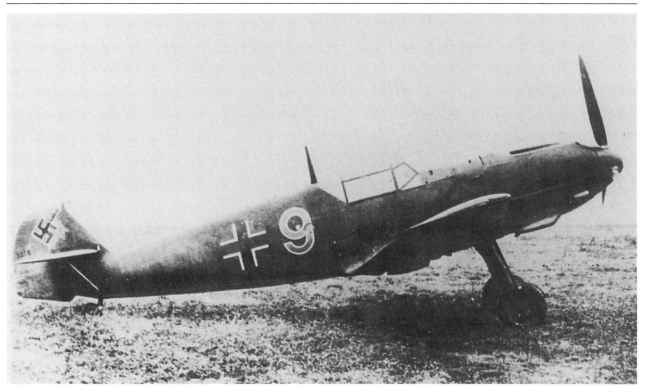

Above: Mid-April 1940 and the *Luftwaffe* had played a vital part in the invasion of Norway. The Emils of II./JG 77 are on the airfield near Oslo with the Ju 52s and Me 110s which had spearheaded the operation. The vertical bar behind the *Winkel* was an unusual addition to the black *Stab* symbols. The *Gruppe* was led by *Major* von Bülow.

Below: *Oberleutnant* Herbert Kroeck was *Staffelkapitän* of 4./JG 53. Here, in November 1939, he is briefing some of his pilots. His aircraft is in the then standard dark camouflage with the *Pik-As* badge on the cowling and the top hat emblem which recalled Kroeck's time with J 88 in Spain. In May 1940, Kroeck was succeeded by *Oberleutnant* Günther Schulze-Blank.

Right: *Oberfeldwebel* Erwin Kley is indicating his second victory, claimed on 22 November 1939 near Saarbrücken. Kley had been one of the pilots who had helped Hannes Trautloft to evaluate the prototype Bf 109s in Spain during early 1937. In 1939, he was flying with 3./JG 2 along the West Wall. Note the line of dark green paint above the tailplane where the fin has been oversprayed with 65 *Hellblau*.

Below: *Unteroffizier* Heinzeller named all his aircraft after his pet dog. During 1940, he flew with 5./JG 3 but he had previously been in LG 2 where he had been a member of the *Luftwaffe*'s official aerobatic team flying Bücker Jungmeister single-seat biplanes. The team performed at several international air displays prior to the outbreak of war.

Above: Bf 109E-1 W.Nr 4859 of 2./JG 2 newly painted in the pale blue scheme. At this time the numerals of second *Staffeln* were still red; in early 1940 they were repainted black. The new camouflage rendered the aircraft less visible against the sky so that attacking aircraft had an element of surprise.

Opposite page, top: Technical Officer on the *Stab* of II./JG 2, *Leutnant* Günther Domaschk in the Emil which is marked with the symbol of his function, a chevron and circle (in German *Winkel-Kreis*). This was in late winter 1940. The pale blue paint on the lower rear fuselage has become unusually discoloured. On many aircraft at this period, the pale paint was allowing the earlier dark greens to show through. (*via Prien*)

Right: Emils of the *Stab* I./JG 77 on Aalborg airfield, Denmark, during spring 1940. The nearest aircraft carries the *Adjutant Winkel* of *Oberleutnant* Kunze and the *Gruppe* emblem on its cowling, the worn-out boot. Raiding Blenheims suffered serious losses at the hands of these fighters.

Above: Christmas time 1939, with the pilots of 3./JG 2 in their dispersal hut. Leaning on the window sill is Franz Jaenisch; above him is Rudi Pflanz and on the right is *Feldwebel* Muller. Yellow 9, in the then newly painted pale blue camouflage, carries the blue and yellow pennant badge designed by *Staffelkapitän* Hennig Strümpell. The identity of 'Motti' is not recorded.

Below: The Technical Officer whose marking can be seen is *Oberleutnant* Werner Pichon-Kalau von Hofe. Both aircraft on this French airfield are from III./JG 51. The black cat badge belongs to 8 *Staffel* which had once been 2./JG 20 before the *Gruppe* became a part of JG 51. The civilian hanger is damaged. Another photograph indicates that there was a bar and a clubhouse away to the right, but the location is not known.

Above: Shot down by a Dutch Fokker on 10 May 1940, *Oberleutnant* Robitzsch crash-landed on De Kooy airfield to become a PoW. He was *Staffelkapitän* of 5./Jgr 186, the fighter unit intended to embark on the half-built aircraft-carrier *Graf Zeppelin*. In the event, most of the pilots joined JG 77 and the carrier was never completed. On the port side below the cockpit is the pilot's nickname *Der Alte*.

Below: Standing by brown 13, W.Nr 1399, on 29 May 1940 at Mont Ecouvez, south of Cambrai is *Oberleutnant* Hasso von Perthes. His left arm is hiding the *Staffel* badge of 3./LG 2 — a Mickey Mouse with umbrella. The Germans always found Mr Chamberlain's umbrella funny. Von Perthes was shot down over Crowhurst by Bird-Wilson (No. 17 Sqn) on 31 August 1940; he died of wounds a fortnight later.

Left: An Emil of 3./JG 2 flying over France in July 1940. Some markings, like the fuselage crosses are still in non-standard forms and the stippled camouflage is unusually dark. It was not until the end of August that rudders, cowlings and sometimes wing-tips were painted yellow or white. (*C. Goss*)

Opposite page, bottom: Men and an Emil of 1./LG 2 hidden under trees on the boundary of a landing ground alongside a French road. Note the three *Abschuszbalken* (victory bars) on the fin of white 9 and the *Staffel* badge that recalled the *Legion Condor* marking — a black disc with an inset white saltire. The two stalks above the rudder are part of the look-out man's binoculars, mounted on a tripod.

Below: Werner Mölders flew this Bf 109E from 1939 until 6 June 1940 when he was shot down by Lieutenant Pomier-Layragues of GC II./7. The aircraft carried a finish typical of III/JG 53. Note the unusual style of the fuselage cross, the *Stab* symbols and the victory markings on the fin. The photograph was taken at Lors, near La Selve, in late May 1940. (*via Prien*)

Opposite page, top: According to General Hrabak, who was the *Staffelkapitän* of 1./JG 76 during May 1940, *Feldwebel* Hager flew an air-test in this white 6, W.Nr 3247, became lost south of Mézières and landed in French territory at Orconte. The aircraft was given French markings and flown by Konstantin Rozanoff who is seen in the cockpit.

Above: Black 11 of 2./JG 3 appears to have lost its propeller and lower cowling in a forced landing. The hood and radio have been interfered with. The Tatzelwurm emblems in 2 *Staffel* were red; in 1 *Staffel* they were white; in 3 *Staffel*, yellow; and in the *Stab*, green.

Left: This is the prototype E-4B bomb carrier. Coded CA+NK it is in the early 1940 pale finish with a spinner that appears to be yellow instead of the standard black-green. Note the wing-mounted 20 mm cannon and the streamlined fairing over the bomb-rack.

Above: *Unteroffizier* Strohauer with his yellow 4 of
3./JG 54. The old dark greens of 1939 have been
oversprayed with a thin grey (02) mottle. The numeral
which previously had a white outline is now being given
a black one. The remains of the *Staffel* badge can still be
seen below the cockpit — a hunter with a long-barrelled
gun. Hangar walls usually carried large notices *Rauchen
Verboten.*

Opposite page, top: This is one of the captured Bf 109s
that were test-flown by the Allies in 1939–40. White 1,
W.Nr 1304, was often depicted in its French colours but
here it is seen as AE479 in RAF dark green, dark earth
and yellow, probably at Boscombe Down. In 1942 it was
sent to USA where it was written off at Chanute Field.
Originally from 1./JG 76, its pilot, *Feldwebel* Hier
returned from captivity in France to his unit only to lose
his life in combat later in the Battle of Britain.

Right: Captured Emil DG200 seen here in 1942 flying
with No. 1426 (EAC) Flight at Duxford. After the war, it
was stored and has now been carefully rebuilt and
painted to resemble its appearance in November 1940
when *Leutnant* Wolfgang Teumer force-landed it on
Manston airfield. It had been an E-3/B, fitted with an
ETC bomb carrier, flying with 2./JG 51. In late 1940, one
Staffel from each *Gruppe* was trained to carry bombs,
much to the pilots' distaste. (*via Bob Jones*)

Opposite page, top: Believed to be at Calais-Marck this was the scene as 3./LG 2 built covered pens to conceal their aircraft. In the foreground, brown 11 had a part of its rudder painted yellow. The speckled appearance is due to sunlight through camouflage netting covered with strips of material. Under the trees in the background is black 11 of 2 *Staffel* with a bright yellow cowling.

Above: A group of pilots from 8./JG 2 waiting for take-off time. On the left is *Leutnant* Willinger; on the right is *Oberleutnant* Mollerfriedrich. Black 2 was usually flown by *Leutnant* Karl-Heinz Metz who collided with *Feldwebel* Goltz over Kent on 5 September and became a PoW. This photograph shows Beaulieu, near Signy-le-Petit during May 1940, early in the German advance.

Left: Typical of the scene on many French airfields during May and June 1940 as the *Luftwaffe* fighter *Gruppen* moved westwards in support of the advancing ground troops. This is probably Charleville, a key location occupied by many units in the course of the French campaign. Here it is occupied by elements of JG 52. Note the I *Gruppe* badge on the cowlings. In the centre can be seen a twin-engined Me 110 *Zerstörer*.

Above: While the second *Gruppe* of LG 2 operated obsolete Henschel Hs 123s in the ground-attack role across northern France, the first *Gruppe*, I(*Jagd*)/LG 2, was already equipped with Bf 109Es; 3 *Staffel* used brown numerals instead of yellow, as on this brown 8. The undamaged propeller blade suggests an engine-off landing.

Opposite page, top: Some of the paraphernalia of a *Gruppe* operating 'in the field'. Yellow 5 (W.Nr 1146) of 9./JG 2 has been festooned with foliage to break up its hard outlines and the highly visible crosses have been covered with sheets. The trucks will have brought up ground crews with tools and ammunition. This is near Signy-le-Petit. It is apparent how warm it was during the second half of May 1940. (*J. Kitchens*)

Opposite page, bottom: *Oberleutnant* Helmut Wick, *Staffelkapitän* of 3./JG 2, prepares to take off from the airfield at Beaumont-le-Roger. The blue and yellow *Staffel* badge can be seen on the cowling. This aircraft was later fitted with an armoured windscreen and the cowling was painted first white, then yellow. Wick flew this machine throughout the autumn of 1940.

Below: This is the elegant Château de Beaumont-le-Roger, the home of La Princesse Caraman-Chimay, Duchesse de Magenta, which became the HQ of JG 2. Today nothing remains; American bombers destroyed most of the little town when they bombed the airfield which was to the north of the *château*. The Duchesse de Magenta and her husband worked for the *Résistance* in 'Alliance'.

Above: This is yellow 3, flown by *Leutnant* Horst Marx of 3./EGr 210, the *Jabo* experts. Marx had to bale out over Frant on 15 August when the unit bombed Croydon instead of Kenley and suffered heavy losses as they withdrew southwards. Note the bomb-carrying gear and the yellow ring on the spinner. Fuselage numerals were painted quite small and close to the cross. (*Otto Hintze*)

Opposite page, top: The fate of many unfortunate Emils that ran out of fuel short of their French airfields. Many aircraft ditched in the Channel but a lot of the pilots glided down on the level beaches. The strong box-like structure of the

cockpit area saved many pilots' lives. Much of the damage to this aircraft of III./JG 51 was probably due to the sea. The pilot may have been *Feldwebel* Bielefeld. (*J. C. Verrycken*)

Opposite page, bottom: When the *Luftwaffe* occupied Merville which had been one of the principal RAF bases in France they found the remains of Armstrong Whitworth Ensign G-ADSZ 'Ettrick' among other wreckage of aircraft destroyed by strafing Emils. It had probably flown in with ammunition and supplies for the BEF and had met its fate before it could evacuate some of the non-combatant servicemen caught up in the great retreat. (*J. C. Verrycken*)

Opposite page, top: Making an engine change using a standard tripod and pulley block was not an unusual event when operating away from a permanent base. Note that the engine bearers have been removed with the engine, as a single unit; note also the hollow prop shaft which had been intended to accommodate a motor cannon, and the semicircular oil tank. No Emil ever operated with a motor cannon.

Opposite page, bottom: White 12, flown by 'Assi' Hahn who was *Staffelkapitän* of 4./JG 2, on a landing ground at Tirlemont, Belgium in May 1940. Personnel are living in tents, equipment lies ready for use and rifles are piled in case of enemy attack. The warm, dry weather during May 1940 favoured the outdoor lifestyle of the advancing *Luftwaffe*. (*via J. Vasco*)

Above: *Oberleutnant* Otto Bertram's Emil somewhere near Amiens in May 1940. It has his 1./JG 2 Bonzo Dog badge on its cowling. Crosses and swastika are still in the positions and style of 1939, though the camouflage colours have been updated to 71/02. The white numeral is outlined in black. (*J. C. Verrycken*)

Below: *Leutnant* Helmut Strobl of 5./JG 27 had to put his black 2 down behind French lines on 19 May. He took a quick photograph and hid in a nearby wood. When German troops arrived, he was photographed with the motor-cycle reconnaissance troops who helped him to return to his unit. He died in combat over Kent on 5 September. (*A. Saunders*)

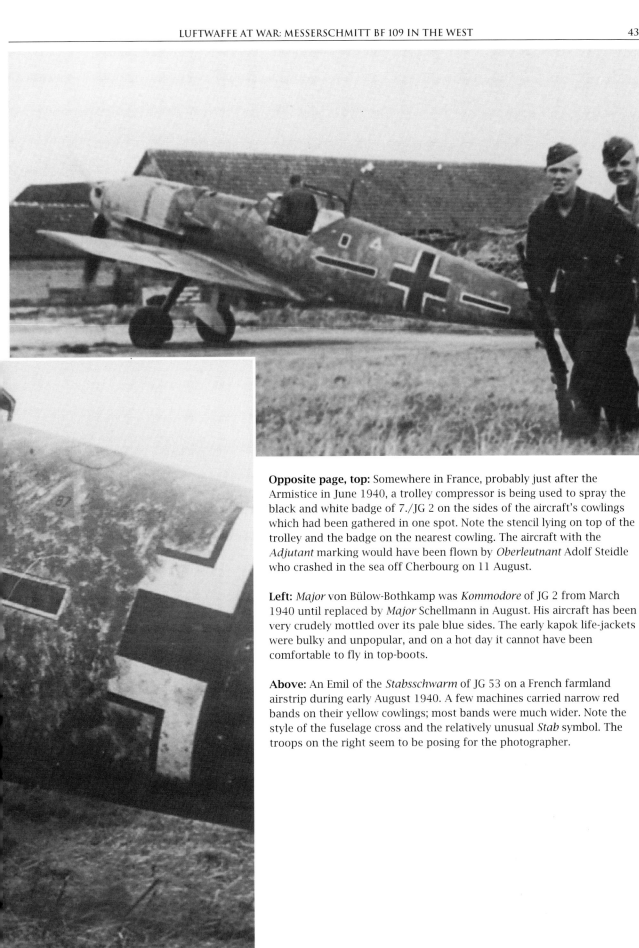

Opposite page, top: Somewhere in France, probably just after the Armistice in June 1940, a trolley compressor is being used to spray the black and white badge of 7./JG 2 on the sides of the aircraft's cowlings which had been gathered in one spot. Note the stencil lying on top of the trolley and the badge on the nearest cowling. The aircraft with the *Adjutant* marking would have been flown by *Oberleutnant* Adolf Steidle who crashed in the sea off Cherbourg on 11 August.

Left: *Major* von Bülow-Bothkamp was *Kommodore* of JG 2 from March 1940 until replaced by *Major* Schellmann in August. His aircraft has been very crudely mottled over its pale blue sides. The early kapok life-jackets were bulky and unpopular, and on a hot day it cannot have been comfortable to fly in top-boots.

Above: An Emil of the *Stabsschwarm* of JG 53 on a French farmland airstrip during early August 1940. A few machines carried narrow red bands on their yellow cowlings; most bands were much wider. Note the style of the fuselage cross and the relatively unusual *Stab* symbol. The troops on the right seem to be posing for the photographer.

Above: Bf 109Es from II./JG 2, in various forms of camouflage, ranged on the unfenced boundary of an unprepared landing ground in France. The nearest machine, with its mottled flanks and white markings, was probably flown by the *Staffelkapitän*, *Oberleutnant* 'Assi' Hahn, who was later to lead the third *Gruppe*. (*via Prien*)

Below: A Focke-Wulf FW 58 *Weihe* such as were used by most *Gruppen* as search aircraft to assist the rescue seaplanes in locating the pilots who ditched in the Channel. Many were used as trainers and as general-duties hack machines and most of them were painted pale grey, with four-letter radio codes. Some versions had an area of transparency at the nose. OZ+AK of JG 51 was shot down over the sea on 11 November.

Opposite page, top: The RAF claimed that these rescue seaplanes were reporting details of convoys. This Heinkel He 59B-2 was brought down on the Goodwins on 9 July and towed ashore at Walmer. Overall white, with black registration D+ASUO, it carries red crosses on wings and fuselage. The tail markings are red, black and white. It belonged to *Seenotflugkommando* 1 based at Boulogne. The pilot was *Unteroffizier* Helmut Bartmann. (*K. S. West*)

Opposite page, bottom: Take-off by yellow 11 of 3./JG 27 from an airstrip in Normandy, probably Plumetot. A new rudder has been fitted, which is still painted in its dark undercoat. On the cowling of both machines can be seen the *Gruppe* badge — a map of Africa with a stylised lioness head. Note the uneven retraction of the undercarriage.

Opposite page, top: August 1940. *Oberleutnant* Priller (centre) is briefing pilots before take-off on the mission during which *Oberfeldwebel* Fritz Beeck was to force-land near Dover. Beeck is the pilot wearing the side cap. The Emil is Priller's machine, marked with his playing card emblem below the cockpit. The *Luftwaffe* always used boundary tree cover to conceal the parked aircraft. (*René Wouters*)

Left: Emils of 8./JG 54 on one of the airstrips around the Forêt-de-Guines. The tree line provided useful cover. The nearest aircraft, with two victory claims on its white rudder, is probably black 1. The spinner is white with a black back-plate and the cowling is yellow. The *Staffel* badge, a red stylised sparrow, appeared on a patch of the original pale blue of the cowling. (*J. C. Verrycken*)

Above: *Hauptmann* Hans Von Hahn was promoted to lead I./JG 3, based at Colembert, during August 1940. The entire nose is yellow with a green Tatzelwurm emblem. The cockerel is by the cockpit and the *Stab* symbols, a *Winkel* and a triangle, are black. This Emil had previously been flown by Günther Lützow. Von Hahn came from JG 53.

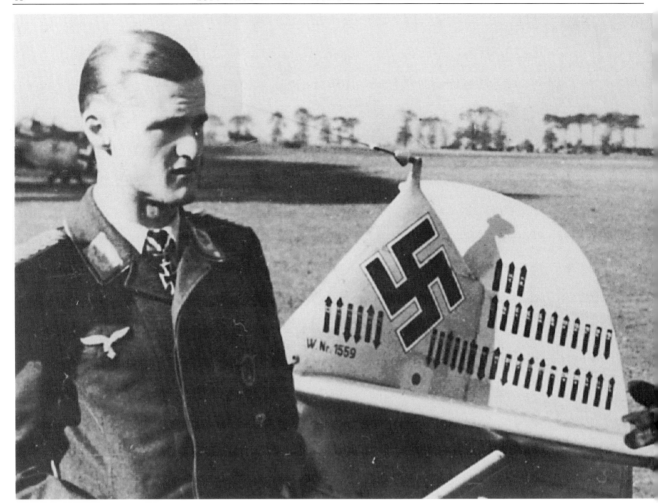

Left: From left to right: *Major* Günther Lützow (*Kommodore*), *Hauptmann* Wilhelm Balthasar (*Gruppenkommandeur*) and *Oberleutnant* Egon Troha (*Staffelkapitän* of 9 *Staffel*), all of JG 3. The aircraft is Balthasar's and the location is the airfield at Wierre-aux-Bois, east of Samer.

Opposite page, bottom: When Wilhelm Balthasar moved from JG 1 to command III./JG 3 he brought with him the Emil, W.Nr 1559, with all his victories recorded on its tail unit. The 'arrows' pointing downwards refer to aircraft destroyed on the ground. Each one is dated. Around the markings, the rudder is painted yellow.

Below: The rudder of Gerhardt Schöpfel's aircraft on 18 August when he claimed four victories. These were marked in black but some pilots of 9./JG 26 marked their tabs in red. Note the triangular area at the top of the rudder which is painted yellow. This is how the ID markings began; by the end of August, entire rudder areas had been painted throughout the fighter force — a most distinctive marking. (*René Wouters*)

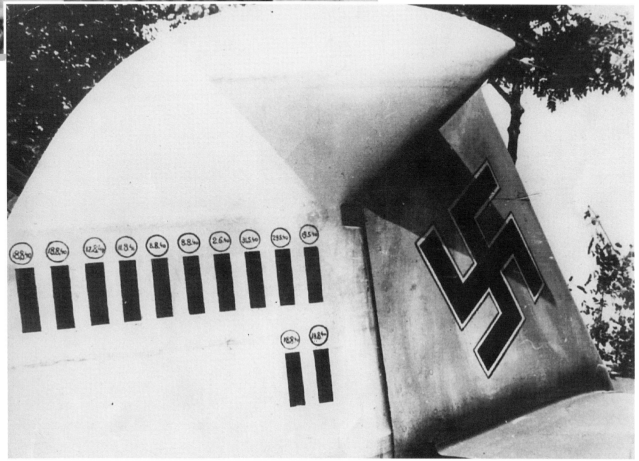

Opposite page, top: Taken at considerable risk by a Channel Islander lurking by the hedge at Guernsey airfield, an Emil of JG 53 roars overhead. The wheels always retracted unevenly. Note the appearance of the red band around the cowling and the slight lowering of wing flaps to assist a rapid climb on take-off.

Opposite page, bottom: La Villiaze, Guernsey was used by JG 53 *Pik-As* as a forward base for their missions over the Channel on convoy operations. This was the Bf 109 of *Hauptmann* von Maltzahn with its *Kommandeur* markings and the temporary red band marking around the cowling. The pilot seen here is *Leutnant* Michalski. Freiherr von Maltzahn later became *Kommodore* of JG 53. (*J. D. Goodwin*)

Above: An unusual photograph, taken on the dispersal area of I./JG 54 in early September. Pilot Officer J. R. Caister's Spitfire, XT-D of No. 603 Sqn, had been forced down on the 6th and had been taken to one of the airstrips south of Guines where it was serviced and repainted in *Luftwaffe* colours. Today, the TGV railway line runs across the wartime airstrip at Campagne-lès-Guines where this incident is reported to have occurred. (*J. C. Verrycken*)

Below: White 2 of 1./JG 3, photographed from a Hs 126 over the coast near Cap Gris-Nez. On 5 October, *Feldwebel* Herwarth von Bittenfeld baled out of a white 2 over Kent. This may have been his aircraft earlier in the summer.

Above: Hans-Joachim Marseille is best known for his remarkable career with JG 27 in Africa. Not so well known is his earlier service with I./LG 2 during which he was involved in several combat incidents. The cowling of this Emil is all yellow; the spinner and propeller were black-green 70. This is probably at Marck in September 1940.

Top right: *Unteroffizier* Keller's aircraft has suffered from a collapsed undercarriage leg while taxiing on a rudimentary grass airstrip in the Pas-de-Calais region. The black numeral signifies that the aircraft is from the second

Staffel of the first *Gruppe* of JG 3, whose red badge can be seen on the cowling. Rudder, cowling and wing-tips were painted white after the end of August 1940.

Right: A salvage team is about to recover this Emil of JG 54 from the French beach where it had force-landed, no doubt short of fuel. Glare from the sun has obliterated the white numeral but the white ID paint on the wing-tip is clearly visible. Upper surfaces are camouflaged grey and green (02 and 71) but the rest of the aircraft is in pale blue (65) for concealment in the air. (*J. C. Verrycken*)

Above: The *Jabo* machines of II./LG 2 were marked with this black triangle. Until 6 September, yellow C had been flown by *Feldwebel* Werner Gottschalk who landed on Hawkinge airfield, wheels down. He took shelter from a trigger-happy sentry in a hangar. The aircraft was examined at Farnborough. It was one of a batch of new E-4/Bs delivered from the parent factory in grey camouflage colours.

Below: Black H of 5./LG 2 is carrying a cluster of four 50 kg bombs on a special rack. The nose is yellow, the triangle and the H are outlined in white and the rudder is yellow. Pilot's head armour can be discerned inside the hood. The *Gruppe* usually painted spinners with bands of (from the tip) white, blue, white and black.

Opposite page, top: A surprisingly large bomb for a Messerschmitt to carry. This is a 250 kg weapon, with an aircraft of 2./LG 2 whose *Staffel* badge recalls the *Legion Condor*. A sheet has been thrown over the cowling to hide its bright yellow paint. LG 2 often painted the entire nose cowling panels yellow, as on this machine.

Opposite page, bottom: Taken during the Battle of Britain, when their rudders were all painted yellow, this Emil is in a camouflaged sandbag pen on an airfield boundary. The pilot, with his five white victory bars, is *Leutnant* Julius Meimberg who flew with 4./JG 2 (and who survives in 1997).

Left: The *Kommodore* (probably of JG 3) who had engine trouble. Somewhere in the Pas-de-Calais area, this Bf 109E lies in the stubble. The cowling is all white and the fuselage has been sprayed with a light mottle of 02 grey-green. It was in this sort of countryside that the fighter *Gruppen* established the airstrips from which they operated across the Channel during the Battle of Britain. (*via Prien*)

Opposite page, bottom: Elements from the first and third *Gruppen* of JG 2 preparing to take off from Cherbourg West (Querqueville). Yellow cowlings and rudders date this photo after the end of August 1940. Different styles of camouflage are visible. The pilot of yellow 5 has put on about 10° of flap to assist take-off from the rather short runway available at this airfield.

Below: White 15 of 1./JG 53 being serviced at Rennes in August 1940. Note the three-tone fuselage colours (from the top 71, 02, 65). This Emil 'belonged' to *Feldwebel* Josef Bröker who had to force-land it at Tatton House Farm, west of Weymouth on 25 August 1940, during a raid on Portland. He recently returned to visit the site where he became a PoW. (*C. Goss*)

Hauptmann Rolf Pingel, the *Kommandeur* of I./JG 26, taxiing out from the dispersal area behind Le Colombier to the main airfield at Audembert. There are seventeen tabs on the yellow rudder, two white rings on the dark spinner and a yellow nose. The row of flags below the hood are of Poland, Belgium, the Netherlands and France. The marking is a double *Winkel*. Traces are visible of the overpainted factory code letters.

Opposite page, top: Replacement aircraft for 8./JG 26 based at Caffiers. Since III./JG 26 retained the pale blue style of finish throughout 1940, each new Emil had to be repainted with small crosses and numerals. This was to help in concealing the aircraft at altitude. These particular aircraft may be factory-fresh or repaired machines that have been modified to become later subtypes, probably E-4s.

Opposite page, bottom: Adolf Galland taxiing his *Kommodore* aircraft into the dispersal area among the farm buildings across the road from the airfield at Audembert. Just visible are the ears of his Mickey Mouse emblem and the Gothic S badge (for Schlageter). The spinner has a black rear ring; otherwise the nose is entirely yellow.

Above: *Unteroffizier* Wolff of 3./JG 52 with his damaged Emil, yellow 15. This unit painted rudders, cowlings and wing-tips white. In this instance, the tip of the tailplane is also white. Cowlings usually carried the *Gruppe* badge, a shield with a running boar. It was not unusual for a difficult landing to result in a collapsed undercarriage leg.

Below: Most of the Bf 109s that crashed in England were collected in scrapyards. This fuselage and engine are seen in a dump near Oxford. Marked with a black 1, it can be identified by elimination as W.Nr 4103 of 2./JG 51, force-landed at Guestling on 7 October by *Oberleutnant* Victor Mölders. At that date the machine was just five weeks old.

Above: Late in November 1940 two aircraft of *Gruppenstab* III./JG 53 prepare to take off from Etaples. The nearer machine is flown by the *Adjutant*, *Leutnant* Schmidt, with seventeen victory claims. Beyond is Wolf Wilcke's *Kommandeur* aircraft with the *Pik-As* emblem visible on the yellow cowling. The *Gruppe* made a political gesture by overpainting the swastikas on the aircraft's fins.

Below: After *Unteroffizier* Leo Zaunbrecher had been taken away to have his wounds treated these troops wandered about ineffectually until an RAF Intelligence Officer arrived to examine and report on the crashed Emil. It was 12 August

on Mays Farm at Selmeston, Sussex. Black 14, W.Nr 3367, had come from 5./JG 52 based near Calais. It was said that a personal camera and film were found in the cockpit. (*A. Saunders*)

Opposite page: An unusual PoW with an escort in London. *Oberstleutnant* Hasso von Wedel was a pilot from World War I who was shot down at Bilsington while flying with JG 3 on 15 September 1940. He was writing the official history of the *Luftwaffe* and was allowed to fly operationally in order to record the realities of World War II combat experiences. He died in 1945.

Left: Late October at JG 3's landing ground above Colembert. This aircraft of 2 *Staffel* is preparing to take off with other Emils. The spinner cap and the cowling emblem are red. This machine is unusual in that its entire fin and rudder appear to be yellow, like the engine cowling. Note the range of wooden aircraft sheds along the boundary in the background.

Opposite page, bottom: Aircraft of 2./JG 3 on the flight-line at Colembert. The airstrip lay along the north side of D224 where a row of sheds had been built. On 22 October, the unit was ordered to fit fairings over tailwheel and spinner apertures. Spinner caps and *Wurm* emblems were red. On black 9 note the single bar on the rudder and the faint remains of factory code letters on the rear fuselage: LH.

Below: Early on 'Eagle Day', 13 August 1940, *Oberleutnant* Paul Temme, the *Adjutant* of I./JG 2 met some Hurricanes from Tangmere and his war ended in this field of stooks beside Shoreham airfield. The spinner tip is pale green. It appears that some previous marking had been overpainted aft of the *Winkel*. Three weeks later, his friend and successor, Max Himmelheber, met the same fate.

Opposite page, top: Sometime in late 1940, Adolf Galland's famous Emil was repainted, though all the old markings were retained. At the same time, a small access hatch was fitted above the foothold and this has not yet been repainted. The fuel triangle is marked 'C3', so an uprated engine using higher octane fuel has been fitted. The line to the right of the cross was caused by a flaw on the negative.

Left: On 12 August, *Oberleutnant* Albrecht Dresz landed this Emil near Margate. He was a member of the *Stab* III./JG 54 whose shield appeared on both sides of the cowling. The blotches of mottle are typical of the unit but not many *Gruppen* displayed white *Stab* symbols. (*Derek Brown*)

Above: Raised on to its wheels, white 2 of 4./JG 52 is parked on Detling airfield on 30 September. *Gefreiter* Erich Mummert was taken prisoner. Cowlings and rudder are yellow. By the windscreen on the starboard side there is a large white disc with a red cat, its back arched. This machine was sent on an exhibition tour around the Midlands.

Above: *Unteroffizier* Bock of 7./JG 26 landed W.Nr 6294F on Camber Farm on 17 September. The suffix meant *Flugklar* indicating that the aircraft had been repaired, and obviously freshly repainted. It is very lightly mottled and the rudder and nose are yellow. The open hatch on the rear fuselage gave access to the radio equipment.

Below: One of the last photographs known of Helmut Wick and the Emil in which he was shot down into the Channel on 28 November 1940. W.Nr 5344 had been his regular machine since 1939, though there is a report that he also flew a reserve aircraft, of which no photographs are known. (*Frappé*)

Above: Holding his Marshal's baton, Hermann Goering came to Beaumont-le-Roger to inspect and decorate the men of his old *Geschwader*, the Richthofeners. His left cuff carries the band with the Honour Title. *Geschwaderkommodore Major* Helmut Wick accompanies the *Feldmarschall* along the assembled ranks. This is late October or early November 1940.

Below: Aircraft from the *Stab* and I *Gruppe* of JG 2 Richthofen ranged at the eastern edge of Cherbourg-Maupertus in late September 1940. In the foreground is Helmut Wick's machine with his double *Winkel* marking; beyond is Franz Fiby's *Adjutant* machine. All the aircraft have yellow cowlings. Wick's Emil has an armoured windshield.

Left: Apparently a new aircraft is being delivered to JG 77 in late 1940. Its *Staffel* numeral will be painted on the fuselage side where an old marking has been overpainted. Centre is *Oberleutnant* Schmidt, *Staffelkapitän* of 9./JG 77; the location may be Cherbourg-West. (*Omert via Prien*)

Opposite page, bottom: Adolf Hitler spent some time on the Channel coast with his fighter units at Christmas 1940. At table, here, he is seated between *Major* Lützow on his left, and *Hauptmann* Keller who was then *Kommandeur* of I./JG 3. The exact location is not known but it is probably at St-Omer. (*Van Dessel*)

Below: Newly delivered to Pihen in October 1940 for evaluation in combat, this Friedrich is having its markings applied. Cowlings and lower rudder are yellow. The rows of *Abschuszbalken* are black and on the fuselage are traces of factory codes SC+GW which have been painted out prior to the application of Mölders' *Kommodore* markings.

Above: Believed to be at Wiesbaden, this is Werner Mölders'
Friedrich in early 1941. The yellow cowling carries the
buzzard badge of JG 51 and the fuselage has been mottled
and given the *Stab* symbols, unusual because of the small
triangle within the *Winkel* which was peculiar to Mölders.

Below: Out of the time scale of the other photographs but of
interest on account of the markings, these Bf 109Fs are
ranged at Beaumont-le-Roger in late 1941. *Kommodore* at
this time was Walter Oesau.